MARVELOUS MAGICIANS

Hello, my name is *Seymour,* the **magicians' rabbit**.

If you want the **inside story** on some of the **best conjurers** in the business, then I'm your bunny! I pop up in all sorts of places in my job (especially top hats), so I'm going to let you in on a few **magical secrets**. But **shhhhhhh!** Keep it under your hat!

THE ART OF ILLUSION

For *thousands of years*, wizards, witches and sorcerers have been a source of mystery, fear and wonder. To discover what magic meant in the past, we need to *travel back in time*...

"THIS IS THE **WORLD'S OLDEST TRICK**. *IT HAS BEEN* **BAFFLING PEOPLE FOR 2,000 YEARS!"**

The cup and balls

1 The magician places a ball under **one** of three upturned cups.

2 The ball appears to **vanish** and **reappear** under another cup or multiplies into **more** balls.

3 The trick ends with the ball **transforming** into a fruit or even a small animal!

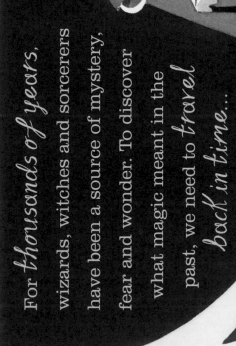

5,000 YEARS AGO
The first magician

On a hot night in **ancient Egypt**, people gather to share the first stories about magic. They tell of a wise wizard named **Djedi** who performed for the Pharaoh Khufu. He cut the head off a duck and then **magically** attached it again. Egyptians also believe that magic can help people to have a happy afterlife.

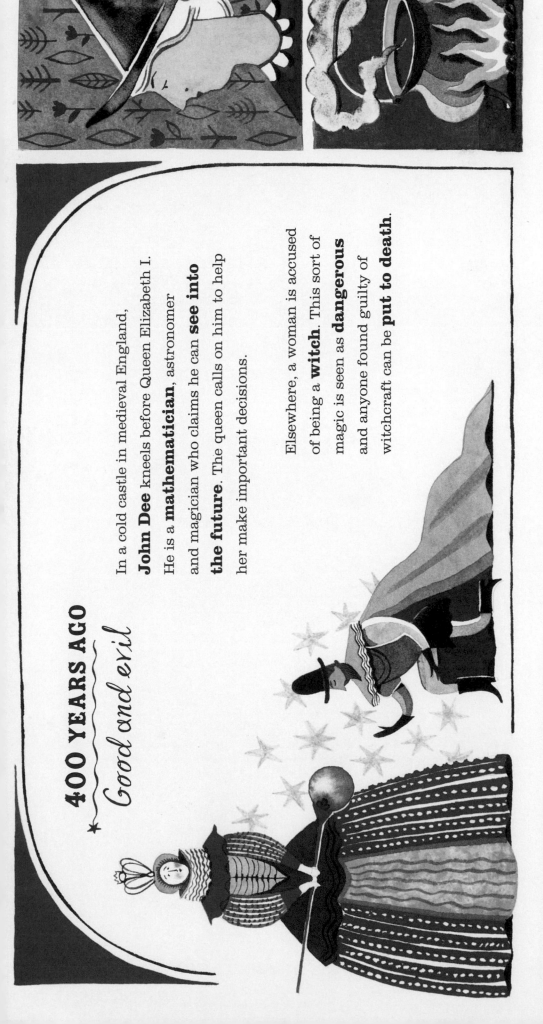

400 YEARS AGO
Good and evil

In a cold castle in medieval England, **John Dee** kneels before Queen Elizabeth I. He is a **mathematician**, astronomer and magician who claims he can **see into the future**. The queen calls on him to help her make important decisions.

Elsewhere, a woman is accused of being a **witch**. This sort of magic is seen as **dangerous** and anyone found guilty of witchcraft can be **put to death**.

300 YEARS AGO
Magical metal

In a candlelit laboratory in England, **Isaac Newton** works late into the night. He is the scientist and mathematician who **discovered gravity**, but tonight he is trying to make a "philosopher's stone." He believes this magical object can **turn lead into precious gold**. Some even think this stone has the power to make people live forever.

IT'S SHOW TIME!

It's a hit!

The orchestra plays, the lights go up and people cheer as a conjurer sweeps onto the stage. *It's 100 years ago,* and magic has turned into top entertainment!

As magic shows grow more popular the illusions become **bigger** and more **extraordinary,** more **daring** and more **dangerous.**

Costumes, props, animals and music are used to create spellbinding effects. Magicians travel the world performing to kings and queens in sold-out theaters. It is the **"Golden Age of Magic."**

MUSIC

ILLUSIONS

ANIMALS

COSTUMES

PROPS

JUST THE TRICK!

Magicians can make us believe the unbelievable.

Before movies or computers existed, magicians invented **special effects**.

They **READ** minds.

You are thinking of a number…

Magicians can pull a **RABBIT** from an **EMPTY** hat.

Ta-da!

They can make things **DISAPPEAR** in a **PUFF** of smoke…

…and with a **FLICK** of a wand, bring them back again.

As if by magic!

They can **ESCAPE** from handcuffs, locks and chains.

They can **CUT** a person **IN HALF** and put them back together unharmed.

Don't be alarmed!

AUTOMATONS

It's over 200 years ago, and *clockwork inventions* are the new craze.

People watch in wonder as these mysterious machines come to life!

Automatons are wind-up machines that appear to work **by themselves**. During the golden age of automatons, **hundreds** of different kinds are invented, from **singing birds** to **mechanical musicians**. They are so popular that people happily pay a **week's wages** to see them.

The POOPING DUCK

QUACK!

An eager crowd gathers.

Families flock to see a small clockwork duck built by **Jacques de Vaucanson**, a famous French inventor.

The **mechanical** duck is the size of a living bird and made from **gold-plated** metal.

As well as **quacking** and **drinking**, it appears to **gobble corn** out of a person's hand, then, moments later, it **poops**.

The audience is delighted!

The MARVELOUS ORANGE TREE

★━━━━━━━━━★

Excitement grows as the talented French magician **Robert-Houdin** takes to the stage. He is about to present his **brand-new** automaton— one of the most **astonishing** illusions of all time.

1 First, Robert-Houdin makes a lady's handkerchief **disappear**.

2 Then he draws the audience's attention to a small **potted tree** sitting on a table.

3 The tree magically begins to **grow orange blossoms** He waves his wand and **oranges appear**.

4 He **tosses** oranges into the audience so everyone can see they are **real**. Then, for the **big finale**…

5 …the last orange to grow **splits open** and two mechanical **butterflies** flutter out, holding the lady's **vanished** handkerchief!

★ INSIDER ★
SECRETS

This illusion is created by *mechanics* concealed inside the tree's pot. It is **wound up** before the performance and real oranges are **hidden** among the leaves. As for the lady's handkerchief—*that remains a mystery!*

THE CHESS PLAYER
An Intelligent Automaton

Meet **MR. VON KEMPELEN**; scientist, engineer and inventor of this talented automaton. **A MACHINE** made from **WOOD, COGS** and **SPRINGS** that works like **MAGIC!**

The automaton taps its fingers impatiently, as if waiting for its turn.

It moves its eyes from side to side, inspecting its opponent.

WHAT?

A life-like chess-playing machine

WHEN?

1769

WHERE?

Austria and all over the world

Hungarian engineer **Wolfgang Von Kempelen** does not see himself as a magician, but he creates one of the **greatest illusions** the world has ever seen. His chess-playing automaton is called the Turk and is unlike any other wind-up machine of the time. It is dressed in a robe and turban and sits at a chess table. Although the Turk seems to be powered by **clockwork**, it can **outsmart** a person! It plays and beats many **famous people**, including Napoleon Bonaparte and Benjamin Franklin.

JEAN EUGÈNE ROBERT-HOUDIN

The Father of Modern Magic

Listen to the **WILD APPLAUSE** as the **SMARTLY-DRESSED** gentleman **WOWS** the crowd with miraculous **FEATS** and modern **MARVELS**.

I can control objects using my mind!

WHO?
The first magician to use science to create illusions

WHEN?
1805–1871

WHERE?
France

He makes his son float in midair.

Robert-Houdin can read people's minds.

Right from the start, Robert-Houdin loves to tinker with **gadgets**. He trains to be a **watchmaker**, like his father. As a teenager, he orders two books about clock-making, but receives two books about **magic** instead. From this moment, he is hooked. He uses his watchmaking skills to build robot-like machines called **automatons**. Soon magicians everywhere are **copying** his modern act and his handsome evening suits.

16

*In fact, **cleverly** hidden inside the table is a **human master chess player**!*

2 Once all the doors are shut, the chess player **lights a candle** in the main compartment. He can follow every move that the Turk's opponent makes by watching the **dangling metal discs** that are connected by **magnets** to the chess pieces on the board above.

3 He keeps track of the game on his own chessboard, then makes his **winning moves** using **levers** to control the Turk's arm and fingers!

Von Kempelen creates the automaton to impress Maria Theresa, the Empress of Austria. He promises her an automaton to top anything she has seen before. Six months later, he returns with the Turk.

AMAZING FACT

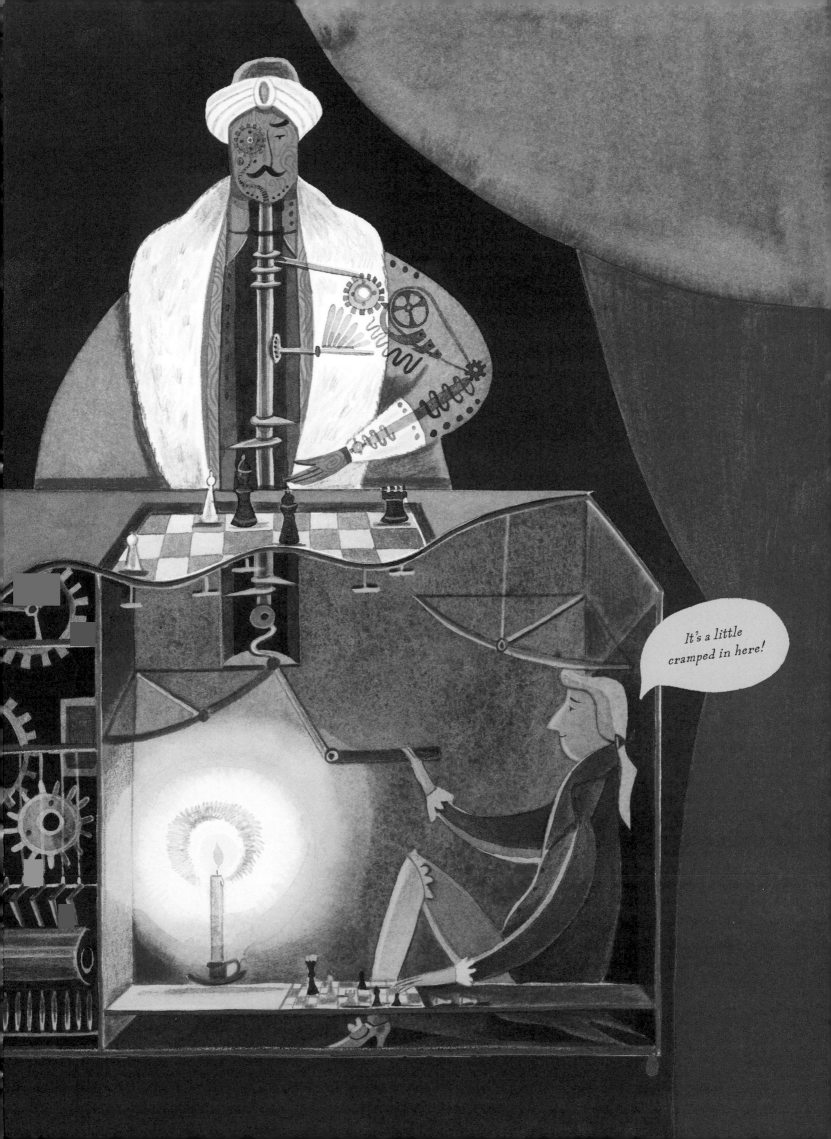

"WHO DARES TO CHALLENGE THE MASTERFUL CHESS-PLAYING AUTOMATON? LET THE GAME BEGIN!"

Well I never, the Turk has won!

TOP TRICK
A Not-So-Simple Game of Chess

1 The front of the chess table is **opened** so that everyone can see inside. Apart from the clockwork machinery, the table looks **completely empty**.

2 The machine is **wound up** and someone from the audience is invited to **come and play** against the Turk.

3 The automaton **clicks** and **whirrs**, then it lifts a chess piece and makes its **first move**.

4 Not only can it play a game of chess from **start to finish**, but it **nearly always** wins!

MAGIC EFFECT

transformation

TOP TRICK

The Light and Heavy Chest

1 First, Robert-Houdin asks a **small child** from the audience to come on stage and lift up a wooden box. She picks it up **easily**!

2 Now Robert-Houdin invites a **strong man** to lift the same box. Try as he might, the man **cannot move it**!

Grrrr! C'est impossible!*

*It's impossible!

INSIDER SECRET

This trick uses the power of **electricity**, which is very new at the time. Robert-Houdin flips a switch and a current runs through a **hidden** electromagnet in the floor. When the power is **on**, the box is **held firmly** in place, but when Robert-Houdin secretly switches it **off**, the box becomes light and easy to lift.

AMAZING FACT Robert-Houdin becomes so famous, he entertains the King of France and the Queen of England!

17

RICHARD POTTER

The Emperor of Conjurers

THE AUDIENCE GASPS as a magician in flowing robes performs UNBEATABLE egg tricks and cooks up DANGEROUS feats.

And for my next trick, I will dip my hand into hot, molten metal.

WHO?
The first great American magician and showman

WHEN?
1783–1835

WHERE?
U.S.

He passes coins through solid tables.

He thrusts a sword down his throat then pulls ribbons out of his mouth.

The son of a slave, who never knew his father, Potter gets a job as a cabin boy when he is just **10 years old** and sails to Britain. He falls in love with the circus and trains as a **tightrope walker**. He discovers magic when he meets a Scottish magician called John Rannie. Potter becomes the **magician's assistant** and learns to do tricks. Before long, he is touring America with his own **sell-out show**.

MAGIC EFFECTS
production
vanishing
teleportation

TOP TRICK
The Enchanted Egg

1 First, an egg **jumps** from the top of one hat to another.

2 Next, the egg **pops up** on Potter's shoulder and **rolls** up and down his arms and body.

3 Where has it gone? The egg suddenly disappears!

Hats off to him!

Cracking stuff!

The Talking Teapot

Potter is a clever **ventriloquist**. That means he can throw his **voice** so that it seems to be coming from **another part of the room**, or even out of a hat or a teapot!

Good evening, ladies and gentlemen!

AMAZING FACT
No one has ever seen a show like Potter's before. Some people are so amazed, they faint!

HARRY KELLAR
The Dean of Magic

The curtains part and there's a BUZZ of EXCITEMENT for the STYLISH magician who has taken America by STORM!

Now for a touch of magic!

WHO?
America's favorite magician for a decade

WHEN?
1849–1922

WHERE?
U.S.

He performs astonishing rope tricks!

He fires his pistol at a lamp and makes it disappear!

Harry starts work at a **pharmacy** at the age of 10. One day, while experimenting with chemicals, he blows a **hole** in the shop floor! Knowing he will be in big trouble, he **runs away** from home. He sees a magician perform at a traveling show and realizes this is what he wants to be. He becomes the **magician's assistant** and travels the world, learning the secrets of magic. Finally he has his own show. The **brilliant gadgets** he invents make his act the best in the business.

"ALL RISE FOR THIS GREAT MAGICIAN AS HE DEFIES THE LAWS OF GRAVITY BEFORE YOUR VERY EYES!"

MAGIC EFFECT
levitation

TOP TRICK
The Levitation of Princess Karnac

1 On a brightly lit stage Kellar's assistant, known as **Princess Karnac**, lies asleep on a couch.

Look! No strings or wires.

2 Kellar makes her levitate— she rises up, **floating** in midair!

3 He then passes a **large hoop** around the sleeping princess, proving she is **held** there by magic.

INSIDER SECRET

Tucked inside the princess's dress is a **flat board** that she lies on. A metal bar **connects** the board to a **hidden machine** that lifts and lowers the princess. The metal bar is **S-shaped**, so Kellar can move his hoop in **any direction** to show that she is floating as if by magic. The dark backdrop and clever lighting keep the working's completely hidden from the audience.

AMAZING FACT Kellar once put on a show for President Theodore Roosevelt and his family.

21

LONG TACK SAM
Master of Magic

WHAT A SPECTACLE! A magician SOMERSAULTS onto the stage, performing BRILLIANT tricks and BREATHTAKING tumbles.

WHO?
The performer who mixes Chinese magic tricks with acrobatics

WHEN?
1884–1961

WHERE?
China and all over the world

His stunning backdrops and silk costumes are specially made in China.

His two talented daughters perform all over the world with him.

As a young boy in China, **Lung Te Shan** grows up loving acrobatics. One day he meets a group of **international performers** who ask him to join them on a world tour. On his travels, he learns the art of magic. He forms his own **acrobatic troupe** and sails to **America** to seek his fortune. Here he changes his name to **Long Tack Sam**. Audiences go wild for his **unusual** mix of Chinese tricks and incredible tumbles.

"FOR HIS FINAL TRICK, LONG TACK SAM WILL PERFORM A SHOW-STOPPING FLIP, THEN BOWL YOU OVER WITH A FISHY FINISH!"

MAGIC EFFECT

teleportation

TOP TRICK
The Water Bowl

I haven't spilled a drop.

1 Long Tack Sam holds an **ornate** silk cloth.

2 He **shakes** the cloth, showing the audience that nothing is **hidden** behind it.

3 He **somersaults** in midair.

4 He lands and lifts the cloth to reveal a **large bowl of water** in his hands.

5 But wait… the audience look closer and see **fish** swimming in the bowl!

AMAZING FACT — Long Tack Sam does acrobatics all his life. He last performs the water bowl trick when he is 73 years old!

23

A MAGICIAN'S TOOLBOX

It takes years of *hard work* and *practice* to create a perfect illusion.

As well as pulling off *tricky moves*, a magician needs special gear, costumes, and a top performance to *captivate* the crowd.

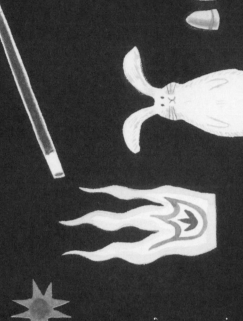

PERFECT PROPS

Magicians use all sorts of props and gadgets, from cards and coins to large animals. Complicated illusions need specially made gear, like trick card decks, coins that separate in two, and boxes with secret compartments. Magic wands help to focus the audience's attention, too.

TOP SECRETS

Shhhhhh! It would ruin the mystery of magic if everyone knew how a trick worked. A magician will only reveal their secrets to another magician—and only if they swear to keep it secret.

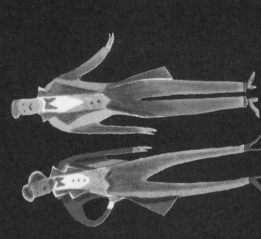

DRAMATIC DRESS

Many magicians wear fancy clothes to impress their audience. Flowing robes and dark cloaks add a sense of mystery.

NIMBLE FINGERS

Sleight of hand is an essential skill in magic. When a magician performs a sleight, they make a natural gesture with their hands to disguise the fact that they are actually hiding something from the audience.

CUNNING TRICKS

Magicians practice the art of **misdirection** to make sure the audience never sees what's really happening. They draw people's attention to one thing, then swiftly do something else without being noticed.

SHOWMANSHIP

The best magicians carefully plan their performance so that it flows from one trick to another, then builds to a thrilling showstopper!

EXTRA EFFORT

Some magicians perform to large audiences in a theater, and others conjure before a crowd on a street corner. No matter where they work, all magicians try very hard to put on an incredible show.

CHARMING CHATTER

When a magician talks to the audience while performing, it is known as **patter**. It is a way of telling the story of a trick. Each magician develops their own style to make themselves stand out.

ADELAIDE HERRMANN

The Queen of Magic

"OOOH!", "AHHH!" The awestruck crowd is caught up in the DRAMA, the DANCING and the incredibly DARING tricks.

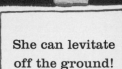

WHO?
The most famous female magician of her day

WHEN?
1853–1933

WHERE?
UK and U.S.

She can levitate off the ground!

She can disappear in a puff of red smoke!

Adelaide first trains to be a **dancer** and **acrobat** in England. She sails to **New York** and marries the great magician **Alexander Herrmann**. When Alexander **dies suddenly**, Adelaide bravely takes over the show. She uses the skills she learned from Alexander to create her own astonishing act. There is **dancing**, music, hundreds of **animals** and incredible **illusions**. She is so **talented** and **original**, she soon shoots to fame.

MAGIC EFFECT

misdirection

TOP TRICK
The Bullet Catch

1 Adelaide invites **six riflemen** to join her on stage.

2 She asks members of the audience to check that the **bullets** and **guns** are **real**.

3 The men load their guns and **fire** at Adelaide.

4 The **smoke** clears and Adelaide is unharmed, **holding** the bullets for the audience to see!

Ladies and gentlemen, please do NOT try this at home!

Ready, aim, FIRE!

BANG!

Great guns!

INSIDER SECRET

Skillful hands **switch the real bullets** in the guns for **blank bullets** without the audience noticing. The real bullets are quickly **marked** backstage to look as though they have been fired, then **secretly** handed to the magician who **pretends to catch** them with their teeth, or on a tray.

AMAZING FACT A single mistake can put the magician in danger. Some have died trying this trick.

27

HARRY HOUDINI
The Handcuff King

A fearful **HUSH** descends over the crowd. World-famous daredevil **HARRY HOUDINI** is **STRUGGLING** to break free from his **CHAINS**.

Nothing can shackle me!

WHO?
The greatest escape artist of all time

WHEN?
1874–1926

WHERE?
Hungary and U.S.

He can escape prison cells, padlocked chests and handcuffs.

He jumps into icy rivers and wriggles out of straitjackets while dangling upside down.

Houdini's real name is **Ehrich Weiss**. He comes from a large family and they are **very poor**. His father struggles to find work so they move to **America** in search of a better life. Weiss becomes fascinated with magic and starts to learn how to **open locks**. At age 17, he **quits his factory job** to perform as a magician. His **hero** is the French magician Robert-Houdin, so Weiss adds an "i" to the end to create his **own** stage name—Harry Houdini.

MAGIC EFFECT

escapology

TOP TRICK
The Water Torture Cell

1 First, Houdini's assistants **fasten** his ankles together in **stocks**.

2 He is **hung upside down** in midair.

3 He is lowered **head first** into the narrow tank **overflowing** with water.

4 The lid is **locked** shut and the curtains are drawn.

5 After **two heart-stopping minutes**, Houdini appears, soaking wet but alive. **Hooray!**

I shall break the glass in an emergency!

I can't bear to watch!

AMAZING FACT

Houdini constantly changes the methods for his escapes to keep them secret and make them hard to copy.

HOWARD THURSTON
The King of Cards

THE KING HAS COME TO TOWN!
Step right up for your chance to watch the MOST SPECTACULAR magic show the WORLD has ever seen.

WHO?
The creator of the largest traveling magic show in the world

WHEN?
1869–1936

WHERE?
U.S.

He is one of the first magicians to pluck a card from thin air.

Everything he touches with his wand explodes into streams of water.

After an **unhappy childhood**, Thurston runs away to join a traveling show. He meets magician **Harry Kellar** and quickly goes crazy for magic. Thurston's dreams come true when he creates the biggest magic show in America—**"The Wonder Show of the Universe."** It takes **eight** train carriages to move all the props and people from place to place. As well as performing many amazing card tricks, he saws ladies in half and makes **all nine** of his assistants disappear!

MARVELOUS MAGICIANS

Lydia Corry

MORE MARVELOUS MAGICIANS

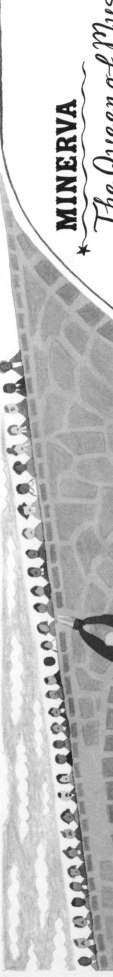

MINERVA
The Queen of Mystery

Minerva is the **first great female escape artist.** One day in Washington, DC, in front of a large crowd, she asks the Chief of Police to **handcuff** her. She then amazes everyone by **jumping off a bridge** into the Potomac River, escaping her handcuffs **in midair.**

WHEN?
Late 1800s to early 1900s

WHERE?
U.S.

WHEN?
1852–1912

WHERE?
Japan

TEN ICHI
Japanese Maestro

Ten Ichi's **thumb-tie trick** is world famous! He invites a member of the audience to tie his thumbs together, then throw **solid hoops** at him. The hoops seem to **dissolve** through Ten Ichi's fastened hands and **miraculously appear** on his arms.

This illusion relies on a revolutionary new method of concealment that takes great skill to perform. To this day, magicians pay for the right to perform this trick, which is why it remains a closely-guarded secret.

INSIDER SECRET

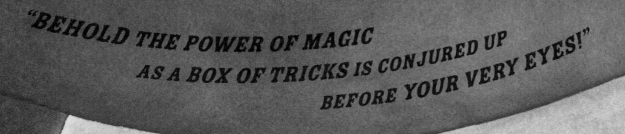

TOP TRICK
The Million-Dollar Mystery

1 Thurston stands beside a small, **empty box** in the middle of the stage.

2 He **aims** his wand... then virtually **anything** imaginable **appears** out of the box!

As you see, the box is completely empty.

It's empty all right!

There's nothing in it.

TALMA
The Queen of Coins

Talma is one of the **most talented conjurers** of her day. She can magically produce **hundreds of coins** from her fingertips. On stage, she wears **sleeveless gowns** so no one can say, "It's up your sleeve!" Her audiences are **astounded!**

WHEN?
1861–1944
WHERE?
UK

MAX MALINI
The Close-up King

Malini performs illusions in **everyday places**. He **borrows someone's hat** for a coin trick, or **bites a button** off their sleeve before magically restoring it. When the **American president** invites him to lunch, Malini snaps his fingers over a **roasted duck** and brings it **back to life!**

WHEN?
1873–1942
WHERE?
Poland and U.S.

DANTE THE MAGICIAN
The King of Magicians

HOORAY! There is a deafening cheer as the DASHING magician, Dante, performs FIENDISHLY good tricks in his LAVISH stage show.

Sim sala bim!

WHO?
Harry August Jansen

WHEN?
1883–1955

WHERE?
Denmark and U.S.

He has a factory where he builds special props for his illusions.

"Sim sala bim" are nonsense words from a Danish children's song. Dante uses them in his show.

When he is six, Harry Jansen moves to **America** with his family. He works as a **prop builder**, then appears in his first magic show **at age 16**. He sets off on a tour, where he is spotted by top magician **Howard Thurston**. Thurston takes Harry under his wing and gives him the stage name "**Dante**." Dante becomes known for his **devilish** looks and astonishing illusions. His extravagant shows include up to **40 performers**. He also appears in **movies** and TV shows.

MAGIC EFFECTS

production
vanishing
teleportation

TOP TRICK
Where do the Ducks Go?

1 Dante presents an **empty bucket** to the audience.

2 He puts on a **lid** and gives it to a **spectator** to hold.

3 He holds up a **real duck** and places it **in a box**.

4 Next he **takes the box apart**, bit by bit. The duck has **vanished**!

5 He then takes the **bucket** from the spectator and opens it. The duck **jumps out**!

Unbeakable!

Quack!

Knock me down with a feather!

INSIDER SECRET

This trick uses *two ducks!* The first duck is held up to the audience, but it is secretly **swapped** for an **inflatable model** before it is put in the box. When Dante takes the box apart, the model duck **deflates** and the box looks empty. The second duck is hiding inside a *secret compartment* in the bucket. When Dante removes the lid, it jumps out!

AMAZING FACT Dante offers $10,000 to any entertainer who can prove they have performed in as many countries as him!

THE ART OF THE MAGICIAN'S ASSISTANT

The assistant climbs into the LONG, WOODEN BOX. Their HEAD, HANDS AND FEET emerge from HOLES at either end. The audience HOLDS THEIR BREATH... as the magician raises their SAW... and begins to CUT THE BOX IN HALF!

NOW HIRING!
Magician's Assistant

RESPONSIBILITIES

- moving things on and off stage

- looking after magic props
  (including animals)

- being a human prop
  (being sawed in half, for example)

MUST HAVE:

- **confidence** in front of crowds
- a **passion** for magic

GENEROUS PAY, COSTUMES AND ALL TRAVEL COSTS INCLUDED!

MAGICAL TEAMWORK

The famous illusionist Howard Thurston refused to step on stage without his assistant George White.

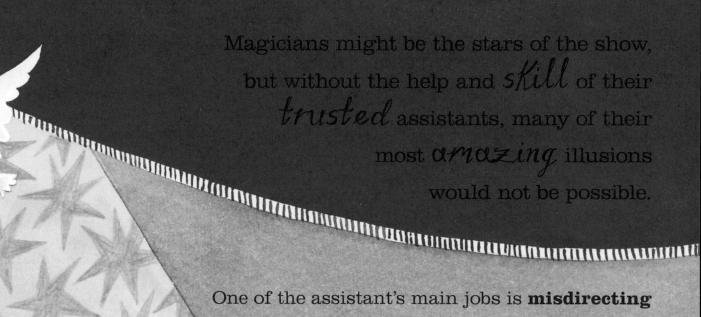

Magicians might be the stars of the show, but without the help and *skill* of their *trusted* assistants, many of their most *amazing* illusions would not be possible.

One of the assistant's main jobs is **misdirecting** the audience, or taking their attention away from the magician. While the **crowd's eyes** are glued to the **assistant** displaying the props, the magician can get away with something **secret**!

A magician's assistant is not always a glamorous lady. **Men and women** can both play this role.

It's not half as bad as it looks!

The bond between Alexander Herrmann and his assistant and wife Adelaide was unbreakable. During his act she was shot at, vanished and even fired from a cannon!

GUARDING MAGICAL SECRETS

Magicians have a hard job to do. Not conjuring rabbits or reading minds, but *keeping secrets!*

No matter how many times a magician is asked how a trick is done, they must *NEVER* tell... or the illusion would be spoiled and the mystery would be *lost forever.*

MANY MAGICIANS' CLUBS HAVE LARGE LIBRARIES FULL OF BOOKS THAT CONTAIN MAGIC'S MOST CLOSELY GUARDED SECRETS.

MAGICIANS OFTEN GIVE TOP SECRET PERFORMANCES TO THEIR FRIENDS AND RIVALS.

MAGICIANS FOLLOW A SPECIAL CODE OF CONDUCT WHERE THEY SWEAR NEVER TO REVEAL THE SECRETS OF MAGIC.

THE SOCIETY OF AMERICAN MAGICIANS

This is the **oldest** organization for magicians. It started back in **1902** in **Martinka's** magic shop in **New York City**. Many legendary magicians have been members, including world-famous escape artist **Harry Houdini**, who was its president.

THE MAGIC CIRCLE

This old, **secretive** society in **London** is where top magicians, conjurers and illusionists meet. To become a member, magicians must first **pass an exam** to prove their skill. Anyone found **revealing secrets** is instantly **expelled**. There is **The Young Magicians Club** too, where junior conjurers can start learning tricks!

THE BROTHERHOOD OF MAGICIANS

Based in **America**, the Brotherhood has more than **10,000** male and female members from **around the world**. Everyone is welcome to join—whether magic is their **job** or their **hobby**. The Brotherhood even has **mini members** as young as seven.

Secret Societies

To protect their secrets, many of the world's best magicians belong to special clubs and societies. These are places where they can share tricks, learn from each other and talk about magic in private.

MAGIC

The art of magic is constantly *changing* as magicians around the world dream up new tricks that are more *daring,* more *dangerous* and more *entertaining* than ever before. Do not try these at home!

VANISHING ACT!
U.S.

In New York, the crowd gazes in wonder as American magician **David Copperfield** makes the towering Statue of Liberty completely disappear.

ELECTRIFYING STUNT!
U.S.

Stunned crowds watch illusionist **David Blaine** for three long days. Dressed in chain mail, he stands on a tall pillar and endures deadly bolts of electricity aimed straight at his body.

EYE-POPPING ESCAPE!
U.S.

Magicians **Penn and Teller** take to the stage. Teller is sealed into a garbage bag filled with helium, the gas that makes balloons float. A blinding light flashes and suddenly Teller has escaped and Penn is holding the floating garbage bag!

FIERY FEAT!
U.S.

Dorothy Dietrich is wearing a straitjacket and hanging upside down from a burning rope hundreds of feet in the air. Somehow she frees herself before the rope breaks!

TODAY

WINNING NUMBERS!

UK

TV audiences watching the weekly lottery draw are astonished as English magician **Derren Brown** correctly predicts all six lottery numbers!

MIRACULOUS MONEY!

China

Close-up magician **Lu Chen** mystifies the crowd by passing coins through a glass table. He invites members of his audience to sit right beside him to prove he is not using any tricks.

ASTONISHING FLIGHT!

Japan

On a brightly lit set, amid laser lights and music, **Princess Tenko** astonishes her audience by appearing to float across the stage before disappearing!

SILKY SKILLS!

South Korea

Yu Ho Jin, the skillful card manipulator, plucks playing cards from thin air, makes them multiply, change color, and then turn into a silk scarf.

BREATHTAKING BREAKOUT!

Australia

Inside Melbourne's aquarium, Australian illusionist **Costentino** is chained to a concrete block and surrounded by sharks and sting rays! He escapes using only a lock pick.

BECOMING A MAGICIAN

Follow these *tips* to take your first magical steps!

3. JOIN A CLUB

Magic clubs and societies are good places to connect with other young magicians. They often organize events and can offer help and advice, too.

Transforming yourself into a magician might seem like an *impossible feat*, but every great illusionist has to start somewhere.

1. PICK A TRICK

Learn one trick and practice it in front of a mirror until you know the movements by heart. Then build up your confidence by performing it for your friends and family.

2. READ AND WATCH

There are lots of good magic books and online tutorials available that teach the basics. You can also learn a ton by watching a professional magician perform live.

> This will do the trick!

4. HIT THE SHOPS

Check out magic shops for specialized gear that you might need, like trick cards and other props.

5. FIND YOUR STYLE

Play around with tricks to make them your own. Develop your own kind of performance and patter.

6. POLISH YOUR ACT

Practice makes perfect! The more you rehearse, the smoother your movements become and the harder it is for the audience to spot how your tricks are done.

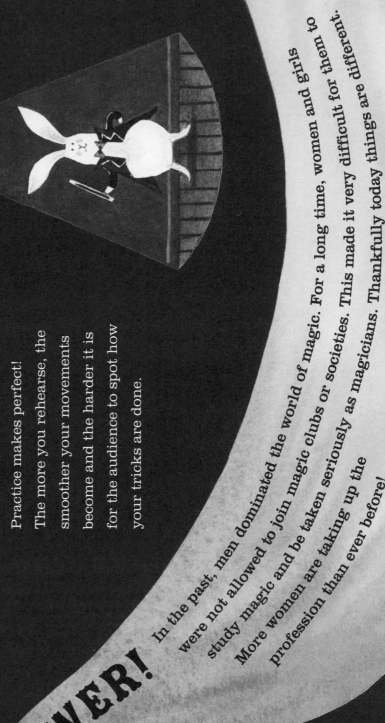

GIRL POWER!

In the past, men dominated the world of magic. For a long time, women and girls were not allowed to join magic clubs or societies. This made it very difficult for them to study magic and be taken seriously as magicians. More women are taking up the profession than ever before!

THE EIGHT EFFECTS OF MAGIC

There are *thousands* of tricks and illusions, but *all* of them are based on one or more of these magical effects. If you want to be a *top* magician, these are the *skills* to master (just make sure you learn how from an expert)!

1. PRODUCTION
making something appear

This is one of the most common effects. Something as small as a card or as large as a person appears to be plucked from thin air.

2. VANISHING
making something disappear

This is the opposite of production. The magician's goal is to make something vanish before the audience's eyes.

3. PREDICTION
seeing into the future

The magician knows the outcome of an event before it happens. They might ask a member of the audience to think of a card, then correctly pull it from the pack, or they may appear to read a person's mind.

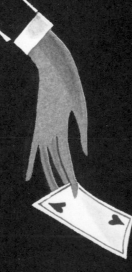

4. TRANSFORMATION
making something change

The possibilities are endless. The magician can change the color of a bunch of flowers or even turn a person into an animal!

5. LEVITATION
making something float or fly

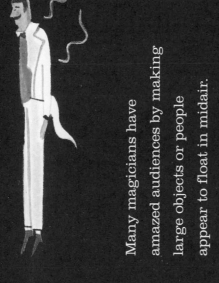

Many magicians have amazed audiences by making large objects or people appear to float in midair.

6. TELEPORTATION
moving something from one place to another

This is when a magician makes an object move in an impossible way, such as passing a ball through the bottom of a cup. When two or more objects move at once, or switch places, it is called **"transposition."**

7. ESCAPOLOGY
the art of escaping

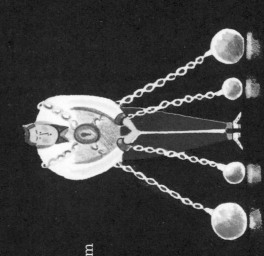

A magician might safely escape from chains, handcuffs, or a locked box.

Unlike other magical effects, the magician doesn't hide this skill from the audience—they just try to escape as quickly as possible!

8. RESTORATION
making a broken object whole again

The magician may cut a rope in two and then magically mend it, or saw a person in half and then put them back together again.

Magicians DISAGREE on the exact number of magical effects. Some believe there are many more!

For Nathan
L.C.

Professional magicians spend their entire careers
perfecting some of the more dangerous illusions
described in these pages, and even then, they can
still be risky to perform! Do not try these at home.

Marvelous Magicians © 2020 Thames & Hudson Ltd, London
Text and illustrations © 2020 Lydia Corry

Copyedited by Cath Ard
Designed by Sarah Malley

First published in 2020 in the United States of America by
Thames & Hudson Inc., 500 Fifth Avenue, New York, New York 10110

Library of Congress Control Number 2020931395

ISBN 978-0-500-65221-3

Printed and bound in China by Reliance Printing (Shenzhen) Co. Ltd

Be the first to know about our new releases,
exclusive content and author events by visiting
thamesandhudson.com
thamesandhudsonusa.com
thamesandhudson.com.au